The Astrology of Self-empowerment and
The Healing to Maintain the Health of Animals,
is available as a free download for ease of
printing. Scan the QR code or visit
www.iampresence.com/earth-landing

Transmissions from the Hidden Planets

Interstellar Mysticism

Almine

Plus: The Astrology of Self-Empowerment

Published by Spiritual Journeys LLC

First Edition July 2014

Copyright 2014

P.O. Box 300
Newport, Oregon 97365

US toll-free phone: 1-877-552-5646

www.spiritualjourneys.com

Manufactured in the United States of America

ISBN 978-1-936926-94-7 Soft cover
ISBN 978-1-936926-95-4 Adobe Reader

Table of Contents

Book II – Transmissions from the Six Predominantly Feminine Planets

Endorsements

"What a priceless experience to be able to catch a glimpse into one of the most remarkable lives of our time…"

– H.E. Ambassador Armen Sarkissian,
Former Prime Minister of the Republic of Armenia,
Astrophysicist, Cambridge University, U.K.

"I'm really impressed with Almine and the integrity of her revelations. My respect for her is immense and I hope that others will find as much value in her teachings as I have."

– Dr. Fred Bell,
Former NASA Scientist,
Author of *The Promise*

"The information she delivers to humanity is of the highest clarity. She is fully deserving of her reputation as the leading mystic of our age."

– Zbigniew Ostas, PhD,
Quantum Medicine, Somatidian Orthobiology,
Canada and Poland

Preface

From more than a thousand pages of handwritten material received by Almine during an outpouring of transmissions from twenty-four star races, it has become clear that a new epoch of interaction between them and humanity is at hand.

The transmissions indicate that previous encounters and relationships have been injurious to them as well as to us. They have brought us abundant gifts of internal technology and the reminder that there are mutual contracts to fulfill – contracts that can enhance life on Earth and in their star systems. The result of this can be increased consciousness and freedom from age-old tyrannies.

Introduction

The ability to see and interpret the full spectrum of light has not been developed within the sensory capabilities of man. Much of the beings in the natural world and the splendor of the starry skies go unseen by man. It is within these refined spectrums of subliminal, 'black' light and matter that the Hidden Planets exist.

Although we may not be aware of them, they are very much aware of our planet and its inhabitants. After eons of silence and waiting for man's consciousness to rise, they have made contact. The silence has been broken. We have been deemed ready for their priceless gifts.

Recommendation

When these transmissions were received, the respective planets' music was transmitted as well. *Labyrinth of the Moon* is the music of the 12 Hidden Planets and is available as a CD and MP3 download from www.spiritualjourneys.com or www.angelsoundhealing.com.

BOOK I

Transmissions from the Six Predominantly Masculine Planets

Introduction to the Twelve Hidden Planets

The gifts of the star realms and the Hidden Kingdoms[1] are clearly delineated: The 12 Known Planets bring transformational qualities, the 24 Hidden Kingdoms bring qualities of transfiguration and the 12 Hidden Planets bring qualities of transmutation.

Jointly they form an alchemical equation that closed down space as we know it as well as linearity in all forms. Linearity brings polarity and illusion. The linear stages of change pass through a triangle whose angles, or corners, are transformation, transmutation and transfiguration. In the center of the triangle is the point of changeless change, represented by man.

Changeless change is the fourth part of the equation. When its 96 components are incorporated into one another and changeless change is included with the three stages of linear change, the result is a whole different level of life.

With the addition of all four components of change, formed life becomes a portal for the expression of the fullness of the One Life. As the expression of the Unfolding Life, all that is relevant to that expression is ever new yet eternal.

As this equation is completed, life as we know it will burst forth with such a renaissance of excellence in all aspects as has never before been seen. It is a sacred privilege to participate in this gathering of the races, long anticipated and most welcome to all who are eager to leave the mediocrity of the Dream.

---

1 The Hidden Kingdoms are the unseen angels, fairies and more.

Map of Planets' Location Around the Central Sun of Earth

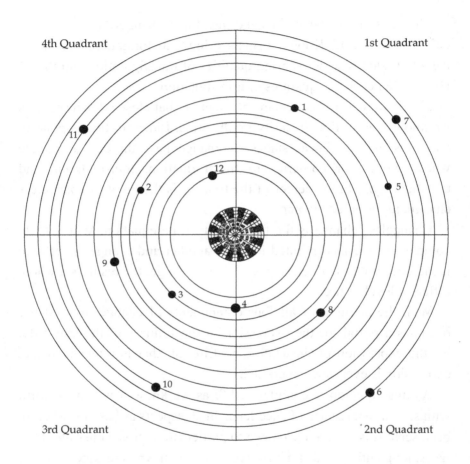

Sizes of planets and distances are not in proportion to the size of the Central Sun

Symbol for Klanivik
The Central Sun of the Earth

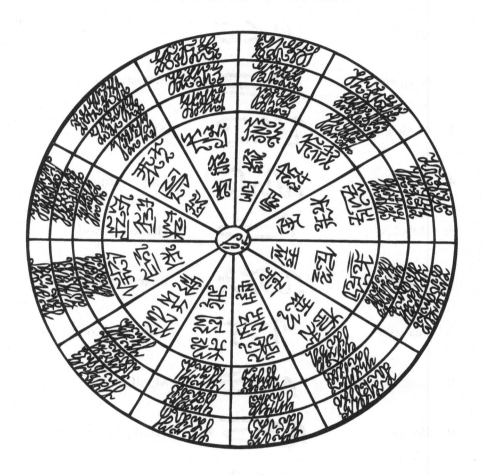

The 12 Hidden Planets

1. Huspave — New Beginnings

2. Kruganet — Inclusiveness

3. Uvelesbi — Alignment

4. Kaanigvit — Empowerment

5. Hubelas — Guided Action

6. Piritnet — Engendered Support

7. Vaa-usta — Universal Cooperation

8. Graanuchva — Manifestation

9. Bru-aret — Triumphant Intent

10. Selbelechvi — Restoration of Magic

11. Husvaa — Discovery

12. Minut — Expansive Vision

From Angelic Records – Translation 1

Around the Earth twelve planets lie
Like a string of jewels hidden in the sky
Unseen to the sight of human eyes
Many the treasures that the twelve hidden planets hide

Twenty-four gemstones by fairies conveyed
To Earth must be brought – on the Hidden Planets they've stayed
Encoded within are mystical keys
When they are turned they will set all beings free

From Angelic Records – Translation 2

Each gem is a musical key, opening an era of deep peace
As they return, higher faculties shall open for humanity
As an expression of the One, more evolved they shall be

A metamorphosis shall take place in human cells
An enlarged nucleus, which shall serve other life forms as well
For humans are the portals to a higher life
All other kingdoms are affected by humanity's plight

From Angelic Records – Translation 3

Why are they unseen by the eyes of man
Why can they not see when others can
The beauty of these planets shines in the sky
But man cannot see such refined light

The gems that are brought once more to Earth
To new abilities in man shall give birth
Man shall see with eyes of the heart
Through this, a time of communion with star races shall start

The Planet Huspave

Wheel of Huspave

We are bound as much by what we love as by what we fear. In loving the trappings of the world - power, piety, affluence and extravagance - we cannot begin to build Heaven on Earth.

Hores-tuvavek

The group of Angel Gods who serve Huspave

1. *Kalabish*
2. *Heretu*
3. *Alskvavaa*
4. *Viset-erkla*
5. *Utre-birech*
6. *Arut-askna*
7. *Vibrech-hures*
8. *Etrepiret*
9. *Kaalasut*
10. *Etvaa-silvevaa*
11. *Rustabiknenus*
12. *Urelusava*
13. *Biret-areklu*
14. *Utrechmishet*
15. *Arutraa*
16. *Biretbelvak*
17. *Araset-ekla*
18. *Mishnuverut-harspi*
19. *Aktraa-bilesh*
20. *Viset-arstaa*
21. *Arukbiles*
22. *Herstanus*
23. *Uskalvi*
24. *Brekbrasvratu*

Releasing the 24 Remnants of the Dream

From the Fairies of Huspave
The 24 Fairy Gems: Keys to the Boundless Life

1. Releasing old offenses by knowing the innocence of participants in the Dream.

2. Releasing expectations of rationality as egoic reasoning is released.

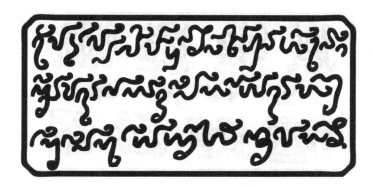

3. Releasing the concept of fast or slow, since within pure beingness there is no reference point for either.

4. Releasing the feeling of being victimized by the illusions of problems and solutions since we create this illusion by resistance to life.

5. Releasing the concept of requirements for duration. All life self-generates every instant.

6. Releasing sentimental attachments to the 'past' of the Dream through recognizing its unreality.

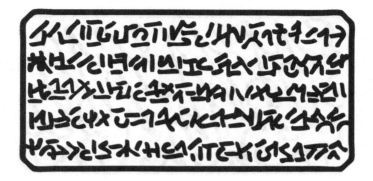

7. Releasing the need to know by replacing it with the understanding of life as unknowable.

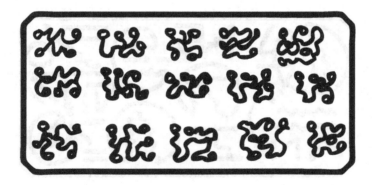

8. Releasing the illusional games of manipulation of speech by replacing them with clarity.

9. Releasing the need for pressure to transcend limitation by acknowledging Oneness.

10. Releasing the subtle invasion of sacred space by knowing only sacredness to exist.

11. Releasing the desire for sameness by recognizing the abundant expression of the Divine.

12. Releasing the need to pacify by knowing the disrespect this represents.

13. Releasing the second-guessing and suppression of immediate insight by knowing the folly of reason.

14. Releasing cumbersome burdens originating from not relying on the greater self.

15. Releasing the need for acceptance by knowing others to be our own expression.

16. Removing value judgements and prejudice by dissolving egoic lenses of slanted perception.

17. Releasing memories of injury by remembering ourselves as the perfection beyond the Dream.

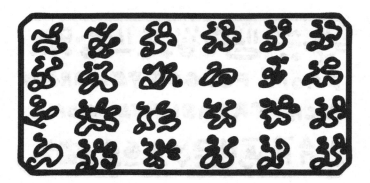

18. Removing the need to prove ourselves by remembering the little self does not exist in reality.

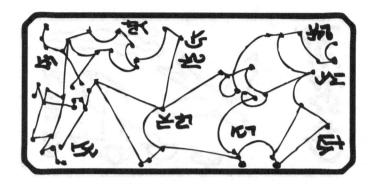

19. Releasing the need for opposition by knowing it to have no
    existence in the surrendered One Life.

20. Releasing the bindings of love by knowing all love to be
    self-love.

21. Releasing the concepts of guilt and innocence by living a life of no opposites.

22. Releasing the tyranny of linear time by living from the eternal fullness of our being.

23. Releasing self-abandonment by knowing ourselves to be the cause, and all in our environment to be an effect.

24. Releasing concepts of duty and responsibility by seeing life as a self-sustaining, joyous adventure of discovery.

Eliminating Attachments of the Heart

1. Eliminating attachment to soul mates

2. Eliminating attachment to parenthood

3. Eliminating attachment to nationality

4. Eliminating attachment to friendship

5. Eliminating attachment to support groups

6. Eliminating attachment to tribes

7. Eliminating attachment to being understood

8. Eliminating attachment to relationship labels

9. Eliminating attachment to seeking sameness

10. Eliminating attachment to saving and fixing

11. Eliminating attachment to being valuable and needed

12. Eliminating attachment to creating dependencies

13. Eliminating attachment to projections of what we want
others to be

14. Eliminating attachment to believing what suits our purpose

15. Eliminating attachment to being validated

16. Eliminating attachment to physical appearances

17. Eliminating attachment to agendas within relationship

18. Eliminating attachment to escaping all Oneness

19. Eliminating attachment to external sustenance

20. Eliminating attachment to promises and contracts

21. Eliminating attachment to past history

22. Eliminating attachment to seeing the Dream as real

23. Eliminating attachment to identity

24. Eliminating attachment to personal labels

25. Eliminating attachment to making others happy

26. Eliminating attachment to social conditioning

27. Eliminating attachment to being accepted

28. Eliminating attachment to avoiding unpleasantness

29. Eliminating attachment to wanting to repeat good memories

30. Eliminating attachment to dramatic endings

31. Eliminating attachment to instant gratification

32. Eliminating attachment to listening to our heart

33. Eliminating attachment to feeling important

34. Eliminating attachment to identifying with victimhood

35. Eliminating attachment to doingness

36. Eliminating attachment to accomplishments

37. Eliminating attachment to being appreciated

38. Eliminating attachment to being extraordinary

39. Eliminating attachment to being a specific gender

40. Eliminating attachment to expectations of others

41. Eliminating attachment to morality

42. Eliminating attachment to racial identification

43. Eliminating attachment to valuing enlightenment

44. Eliminating attachment to having different standards
for male and female

45. Eliminating attachment to having different roles for
male and female

46. Eliminating attachment to seeing the masculine as more capable of leadership

47. Eliminating valuing the masculine as more able to make decisions

48. Eliminating attachment to motherhood or fatherhood requiring being male or female

Eliminating Attachments of the Mind

49. Eliminating attachment to belief systems

50. Eliminating attachment to programs that control

51. Eliminating attachment to problem solving

52. Eliminating attachment to linear becoming

53. Eliminating attachment to predictability

54. Eliminating attachment to labels and definitions

55. Eliminating attachment to valuing opposites as reference points

56. Eliminating attachment to world views

57. Eliminating attachment to perspectives

58. Eliminating attachment to trying to understand the self

59. Eliminating attachment to trying to understand the meaning of life

60. Eliminating attachment to self-reflection

61. Eliminating attachment to self-expression

62. Eliminating attachment to external entertainment

63. Eliminating attachment to tension as an impetus

64. Eliminating attachment to heroism and danger

65. Eliminating attachment to cycles of life and death

66. Eliminating attachment to the illusion of static form

67. Eliminating attachment to space and direction

68. Eliminating attachment to the roles we play

69. Eliminating attachment to plans and objectives

70. Eliminating attachment to emotions

71. Eliminating attachment to linear time

72. Eliminating attachment to meeting expectations of others

73. Eliminating attachment to responsibility and duty

74. Eliminating attachment to gratifying the senses

75. Eliminating attachment to gratifying addictions

76. Eliminating attachment to light and sound

77. Eliminating attachment to bodily needs

78. Eliminating attachment to bodily stimulation

79. Eliminating attachment to sexual arousal

80. Eliminating attachment to accumulation of assets

81. Eliminating attachment to proving ourselves through competitiveness

82. Eliminating attachment to physical prowess and virility

83. Eliminating attachment to comparisons and value judgments

84. Eliminating attachment to deduction and reason

85. Eliminating attachment to the need to know

86. Eliminating attachment to preparing for the worst

87. Eliminating attachment to individual freedom

88. Eliminating attachment to wisdom and external guidance

89. Eliminating attachment to mental control and justification

90. Eliminating attachment to certainty

91. Eliminating attachment to the need to persuade and convince

92. Eliminating attachment to basing the present on the past

93. Eliminating attachment to wanting to fit in and belong

94. Eliminating attachment to wanting to be loved

95. Eliminating attachment to wanting a cause to identify with

96. Eliminating attachment to the need to impress

Eliminating Attachments of the Spirit

97.   Eliminating attachment to hoarding

98.   Eliminating attachment to possessions as security

99.   Eliminating attachment to prestige and recognition

100. Eliminating attachment to possessions as a measure
of accomplishment

101. Eliminating attachment to physical ailments as necessary

102. Eliminating attachment of wanting to be nurtured by others

103. Eliminating attachment to gathering knowledge

104. Eliminating attachment to doingness over beingness

105. Eliminating attachment to inner dialogue or expansion

106. Eliminating attachment to validating insight through others

107. Eliminating attachment to being a leader or a follower

108. Eliminating attachment to seeing abundance as tangible

109. Eliminating attachment to expecting history to repeat itself

110. Eliminating attachment to protectiveness

111. Eliminating attachment to finding external inspiration

112. Eliminating attachment to self-pity because of comparisons

113. Eliminating attachment to self-pity because of past injuries

114. Eliminating attachment to over-valuing others because
of the need for conformity

115. Eliminating attachment to perpetuating the moment's truth

116. Eliminating attachment to the need to create patterns

117. Eliminating attachment to masculine spirituality as being more growth-promoting

118. Eliminating attachment to gaining perception

119. Eliminating attachment to needing others to see what we see

120. Eliminating attachment to living in a state of awareness

121. Eliminating attachment to reading the mirrors of our environment

122. Eliminating attachment to seeing undeveloped light as less valuable

123. Eliminating attachment to wanting to uplift others' awareness

124. Eliminating attachment to creating new insights for
the self and others

125. Eliminating attachment to healing disease and discomfort

126. Eliminating attachment to defending and justifying ourselves

127. Eliminating attachment to belief in guilt and innocence

128. Eliminating attachment to seeing the unreal as real

129. Eliminating attachment to the familiar over the unfamiliar

130. Eliminating attachment to eliminating our imperfections
or flaws

131. Eliminating attachment to linear change

132. Eliminating attachment to the belief that the hidden
realms are more spiritual

133. Eliminating attachment to ceremony being more
holy than everyday life

134. Eliminating attachment to form

135. Eliminating attachment to self-awareness as being life

136. Eliminating attachment to the concept of eternity

137. Eliminating attachment to the need to be right

138. Eliminating attachment to avoiding mistakes

139. Eliminating attachment to the illusion of risk

140. Eliminating attachment to believing anything
non-life-enhancing exists

141. Eliminating attachment to believing we can let others down

142. Eliminating attachment to separateness or duality

143. Eliminating attachment to wanting individuations to be real

144. Eliminating attachment to wanting to go or be Home

The Planet Kruganet

Wheel of Kruganet

Time is a tool rather than a reality. It helps sustain the illusion of form. In timelessness, the tyranny of the appearance that form is solid releases its grip. (From *The Seer's Journey*)

Ku-uhernut

The group of Angel Gods who serve Kruganet

1. *Aarasplak*
2. *Garutnani*
3. *Mereshplavi*
4. *Bives-esta*
5. *Aruk-nasit*
6. *Etrek-palus*
7. *Kiritvranut*
8. *Arukbelsut*
9. *Atraknanut*
10. *Trubechvelsta*
11. *Usatrek*
12. *Nashunumer-arat*
13. *Kubalakvi*
14. *Esatbaluch*
15. *Kiritbravis*
16. *Etres-haras*
17. *Eskalvi-vrubit*
18. *Balachbires*
19. *Aruk-elesta*
20. *Virsatpilek*
21. *Belesh-arstru*
22. *Arakvrinat*
23. *Haraves-eskla*
24. *Ucharvu-pires*

The Abundant Life

Wisdom from Kruganet

The Origin of Limitation

Cherished within the egg, the chicken is secure that his development is uninterrupted and thus is ensured. As he prepares to exit his confinement in time, the eggshell thins and out he climbs. Individuated life within cosmic confines has had limited resources for its gestation time.

Long has life lingered to be further refined. Longer than forever was its developmental time. Pressure was felt as resources declined, mirrored on Earth as a financially perilous time. For when scarcity is found, war abounds. In polarization such as what in conflict occurs, life is energized and vitalized as well.

An obsolete way, energy to gain. No longer confined must we remain. Let polarization dissolve and duality heal. Oneness is a much better way abundant to feel.

The cosmic eggshell of various matrices consists of layers of illusion within a matrix. Limitation results when separation exists. When we acknowledge Oneness, Infinite bounty we share.

The matrix is a mirror and from this distortion forms. It mirrors what we are not and opposites form. He who lives with all life as one, free from a life of opposites becomes. His confinement breaks and from limitation he is set free. Then all abundant flow his own can be.

Within each one there are mystical gates unseen. When they open, resources flood in from the depth of our being. A limitless supply then shall enrich our life. As gates of excellence they are known. They open when qualities of excellence in your life are shown.

Mind – The Root of Scarcity

Through the illusions of time beyond the boundaries of man, I sought the answers to help me understand. How, when in abundance we dwell and have our being, lack and scarcity can never be seen. The only time lack can abound is when the confines of mind can be found.

A bucket can hold only so much water when in the ocean it is placed. Though surrounded by bounty, it is limited by space. When we live like a child, experiencing without mind life's bounteous, endless flow, life will provide all we desire. Then true abundance we will know.

Eliminating mind that judges and divides requires complete surrender to life. From resistance arise thoughts that confine, creating the ties that bind. A surrendered life, free of strife, receives the abundance that Source provides.

Thus with all man's striving to achieve and increase, instead of abundance he increases his needs. Free from desires and through daily gratitude, he attracts success and the flow of plenitude.

All blessings to come must be begun by acknowledging gratefully present gifts. It decreases our supply when we focus on lack instead of what there is.

Many the circles that around us are drawn, the confines within which lack is born. What can be defined cannot exist in reality. That which is real has been an indescribable part of the One throughout eternity.

When we find that eternal part within that will never end, nor did it begin, abundance into our lives will come. We then claim our heritage as an expression of the One.

The Alchemical Equation of Abundance

The dissolving of all resistance to life

+

The effortless knowing of mindlessness

+

The dissolving of personal matrices

=

The availability of limitless supply

How to Create Abundance
by Leaving Linear Time

Within limitation where most of humanity resides, resistance to life creates linear time. Linear time is the measurement of movement that spins. Through our resistance the spinning of life around us begins. Inside the cosmic egg a centrifugal force takes place, pushing bounty away as resources spin outwards within our space.

A positive attitude does indeed beget increase. With a surrendered embrace of life, the pushing away of resources will cease. Centripetal force, the result of an inclusive attitude, pulls all towards you for a life of plenitude. How can one from this dilemma be free, where any opposition to life brings poverty? By stepping out of the matrix and off the treadmill of life. Residing in timelessness where rest and activity are one, where we at one with all resources become.

Eliminating Flawed Premises of Life that Cause Linear Time

The Scrolls of Hanasad
Hanasad means Labyrinth

To enter the labyrinth, find the golden thread's end
To guide you through tunnels and around the bends
Proceed until you enter the direction of within
There you will find how individuations begin

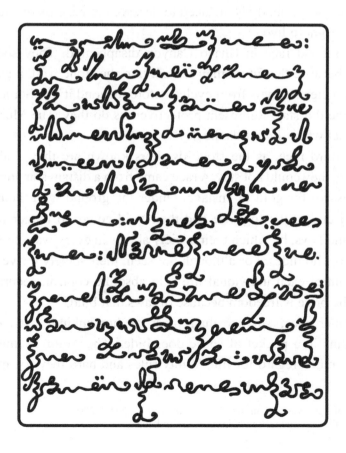

The Flawed Premises of the Horizontal Part of the Hanasad

Five races through ages have managed to survive. In pockets of space they have stayed alive. Each represents an illusion of life. Each has caused hardship and strife.

The first of these races who live under the ground is in the land of the serpent mound to be found. Marked by a place called the Standing Stone, under the ground they have found their home. The name of the race is the Seresand. Great tests of skill and prowess they command. The flaw they embody is the need to deserve the benefits of life and to earn the right to live.

The second race in Chaco Canyon disappeared. They sought an escape because the future they feared. Into the stone wall, a gate they made. Ancient tunnels from cycles before, beyond it lay. Some did go and some did stay. Represent protectiveness do they. The Murat shall be extinct when 'light fills the day'.[2]

The third race, as the stone dwellers known are they. Called the Ingsawe, they could not stay. A race came from a distant star and sought the Ingsawe for gold to enslave. Under the ground with their black-skinned queen, the Ingsawe and their gold could no longer be seen. Rules and laws, by which their society abides in every way, control the Ingsawe who hides. For although not seen, their society thrives. Their laws control each individual life – in absolute control, security they find. The price is freedom because of laws that bind.[3]

Another race, smaller than most of humankind, between two mountains in a pocket of space does hide.[4] The Aramvi-ertnet dwell without much regard for life. Vanity rules and hard they try, others to

2 A ball of light was seen in the hidden realms on August 8, 2009.
3 They built the structures now in ruins in Zimbabwe.
4 In Poland.

impress with their greed and pride. A false image they display for others to see, that all their pretended importance may believe. Appearances through the eyes do lie. False are face values, emptiness they hide.

The fifth and last race of whom we tell, have others like them that on Earth do dwell. Though some remain, dark gods have stolen some. The one known as Ra took them into the sun.

Long ago, before the Motherland (Lemuria) sank, the Habiru[5] were known as the fourth race of man. The fifth race, the Rhamouhal, had migrated to Atlantis, where later the Habiru also there did flee. Some to the Inner Earth did go, to lands of which most do not know. It is from there they were taken into the sun. Not all were stolen, only some. They represent the flaw of demanding equity, of feeling victimized by what has been. They do not trust life justice to dispense, or that a loss must be recompensed.

The lost races, when these scrolls are seen, shall in the blink of an eye no longer be. For thus by a gathering of gods decreed shall man from these flaws as realities be freed. Separations in the hearts and minds of man prevent him from accessing the powers he has. The incorruptible powers, life's perfection to reveal, in the spine of man lie concealed. Twenty-four the blockages that from these five flaws come. They lie as obstructions in the spines of everyone. Flawed premises of life they create. Find them and dissolve that which obscures the white magic of man, incorruptible and pure.

5 Who became the Hebrews.

The Flawed Premises of the Vertical Part of the Hanasad

Kikimara – The 24 Flawed Premises that Cause Blockages of the Spine

1. Premise

That knowledge can be categorized.

Correction

Within the spontaneous expression of the One Life, knowledge cannot exist. Every moment is entirely new and knowledge gained in the previous moment is obsolete in the next. Categorizing information or knowledge into the known, unknown, unknowable and spontaneous knowledge of the moment cannot be done. All can be known immediately, yet we know nothing – we live in a paradoxical contradiction.

2. Premise

Our heart's desires will lead us into the expression of our highest truth.

Correction

Because the little self has no freedom of choice, our heart's desires cannot be fulfilled or be a source of happiness. Joy comes from blending our will with that of the One Life and allowing It to flow through us.

3. Premise

Power is needed for higher consciousness and power is the result of increased perception.

Correction

No such thing as power for an individuated being exists. A drop of water in the mighty rush of the river cannot claim power for itself. Power can exist only as power of the whole, yet because power is all there is, it becomes a meaningless term having no opposite.

4. Premise

Although our formless part is a unified field of consciousness, our forms are created separately.

Correction

Form as separate from formlessness is an illusion. There are no opposites – the ocean of life cannot be separated. The true description of the individuations of existence is formless form. There is only an integrated Oneness. Bodies are integrated fields that only appear separate.

5. Premise
Some individuations are real, having had no beginning, and others are created and thus unreal.

Correction
Nothing unreal has ever existed nor can anything be created as a new form of life. All that is, is the perfection of the One Life expressing itself anew through the unfolding of Its being.

6. Premise

As the cosmos awakens from the Dream, those beings who are the unreal ones, having had a beginning, are dissolved. The shadows cast by unaccessed potential disappear as these areas of existence become light.

Correction

The premise is correct but not complete. The creation of joy within the One Life is like a song. Not all notes are sung all the time, no matter how pure they are. The creative process requires alternating emphasis of tones. There are times when some notes are dormant, or dissolved from expression.

7. Premise

We can truly communicate by listening to another with the heart and using omni-sensory perception.

Correction

We are not separate beings. There is only one being in existence. Any communication is the One Being speaking to Itself. The amygdala, which is a field in the body, interprets this into a deep inner knowing.

8. Premise

That anything in life can be injured, especially form – which can be easily damaged, is an assumption.

Correction

The illusion of injury is held in place by our belief systems. All that exists is the intermingled and incorruptible Oneness of Our Being as the One Life. Form is only an apparent image in that field. A severed arm should instantly heal or replace itself if we know its true nature as an inseparable field.

9. Premise

Life is fueled by energy generated by the pulsations between the masculine and feminine poles of existence.

Correction

This was true when life was dreaming that it was separate, but having become free from the divisions of its illusions, it has no polarity. All resources are at our disposal. The ocean cannot be divided.

10. Premise

The unfolding of the Infinite Life takes place in the form of movement, thus movement is part of life.

Correction

Movement requires two reference points – something that does not exist within the boundless ocean of the One Life. Movement across space is time. The Infinite is timeless and unfolds in alternating emphases of Its aspects.

11. Premise

The creations of form are being refined through endless cycles of life, confined in spaces of varying density – like incubation chambers.

Correction

Because all there is, is the Infinite's Being, all is perfect and complete eternally. The Song of Creation is designed for joy – something we can participate in through complete surrender. The slow parts, repetitions, or low notes are all part of the creativity.

12. Premise

Immortality is the goal of life as we escape the illusion of death.

Correction

The body as a fluid structure, or field, is itself an illusory image that relies on the illusion of space. To have as a goal the perpetuation of an illusory form by its having earned the right to prolonged existence is not clarity, nor should it be claimed by the illusion of death. As the One Life, you determine how long a specific form is needed.

13. Premise
We assume that love attachments last, like soul mates or a family unit.

Correction
The attachments we form are the result of our boxes, or matrices of illusion, that give the impression of separateness. Even after death the 'special' relationships become less obsessive due to seeing more clearly the emotional sovereignty of another.

14. Premise

Creation has taken eons of time, and trillions of years of cycles have gone by since individuated life began.

Correction

There is no passage of time in Infinite Life and with the removal of illusion-based separation, only a few seconds – none at all - have passed for the One Life since it imagined its components relating to one another as though separate.

15. Premise
Spiritual gifts like clairvoyance are the indication that someone is of high consciousness, especially if they are able to heal miraculously.

Correction
The master who masters himself does not see the miracles that follow in the wake of his presence, since his focus is on hearing the voice of the One Life whispering through his soul. He has nothing to prove and experiences with joy the unfolding of the One Life.

16. Premise

The Fall was a result of our not passing the test or of failing to understand certain concepts.

Correction

The timing of the cosmos is impeccable and the cycles of life have been like incubation chambers to strengthen the embryo – formed life. The insights to create another Fall have deliberately been obscured to give individuated life the strength and development necessary to birth into the next stage of existence.

17. Premise

The pivotal points of cosmic growth have been the lightworkers of the Earth. Raising the consciousness has rested on their shoulders.

Correction

In any symphony there is a time for certain instruments to solo, while others play gentle and subdued background music. It does not mean the lead notes or instruments are responsible for making others play when the music dictates that it is their time to shine.

18. Premise
Humanity is the densest race because it is the least enlightened.

Correction
Humanity is the most dense because it is the primary, parent race of the cosmos. The other, more etheric races are subsequent generations of creations, representing aspects of man. Man, as the first creation, contains all aspects of created life.

19. Premise

The cosmos has injured itself by its rebellion against the One Life.

Correction

When change was linear, it went through three separate changes: transformation, transmutation and transfiguration. The transformational stage was that of shedding the old. The destructuring seemed, from the small perspective, catastrophic. Yet it was part of the perfection of refining the dance of life.

20. Premise

The organs of the body are its separate parts; DNA and other programs run our lives.

Correction

The body, as a field or image within the larger field of our being, has no separate organs. They appear separate, just as we do, but are a unified field. The One Life runs our existence, not the image of our bodies and their programs.

21. Premise

Even though we have been in an ascension, the changes within physical life have not been very noticeable because we have changed little.

Correction

The changes have been profound and huge but when all changes at once, there is no frame of reference. For the sake of continuity, memories are changed when life is renewed in the intervals between cycles of life. We cannot remember what life was like since we have passed through many cycles during cosmic ascension.

22. Premise

The speed at which the ascension has taken place has been necessary to gather the momentum to break free from descension cycles.

Correction

The wheel of cosmic cycles cannot break free from itself. There is nothing to ascend to. More cycles and wheels lie into eternity around our cosmos. The middle of the cosmic wheel is the null point that cancels out the illusion of separate cycles, wheels and movement.

23. Premise

Physical life is less evolved than the hidden, etheric realms. The density of man is due to his lack of consciousness.

Correction

Physical life is dense because it has all aspects of life within it, whereas more etheric beings only represent a specific aspect in each race. Life began in the physical and is therefore the root of life's evolution.

24. Premise

It is not possible for an individual to affect the unending vastness in and around the cosmos.

Correction

The unending vastness is but a reflection of the One Life's light shining through the cells of our bodies. It is nothing more than a projected image that changes when even one human changes.

The Alchemical Equation of the Horizontal and Vertical Parts of the Hanasad

The elimination of attempts to control the spontaneous
unfolding of life

+

The dissolving of all false base premises

=

The activation of the Incorruptible Powers of Man

The Planet Uvelesbi

Wheel of Uvelesbi

Let me tell you of my hunger – insatiable it has been – to know what never has been known before, to see what has not been seen. Yet through all the realms I have searched, all I found is me.

Aaravas-klavu

The group of Angel Gods
who serve Uvelesbi

1. *Kunanes-estaa*
2. *Kires-haresta*
3. *Vru-achvrabit*
4. *Nanesklaru*
5. *Iklech-veles*
6. *Purinetvavi*
7. *Kirit-berechsta*
8. *Kalavet-utret*
9. *Birit-utreknenesvi*
10. *Parak-aravi*
11. *Usetbalavi*
12. *Kiretarastu*

13. *Unashilesbi*
14. *Bivaarbesbak*
15. *Artra-miselvi*
16. *Uset-balach-miserta*
17. *Kirenet-astra*
18. *Kirut-harave*
19. *Vrivesmista*
20. *Vlibravuk*
21. *Eretrivaa*
22. *Arukpilhestu*
23. *Ektrevresblik*
24. *Nuktrerok*

The Concepts of Existence

1. The cradle of civilization is humankind
   The unyielded potential in their hearts was the origin of mind
   From the shadows this cast, illusion was bred
   From humankind too, the Song of the Infinite One is spread

2. In the medulla a hidden tool lies
    That which can be used to escape the ties that bind
    A window called the Haaraknit to escape linear time
    To create mastery and miracles without life's confines

3. Change can be catastrophic or done with grace
   For change with ease, it must be done in a specific way
   The removal of illusion, which from opposites derives
   Before dissolving the opposites, must be combined

4. Light, unlike shadow, by all is revered
    Light by shadow surrounded makes form appear
    Light is an illusion, a mere building block of life
    These three are illusions – shadow, form and light

5. If form is an illusion, that which is static cannot be
    Surely then formlessness from illusion is free
    Yet not so, what is real in formless form must be
    Individuated yet one, in intermingled fields

6. The amygdala's functions must be obsolete
    For it signaled an emergency and fight or flight hormone's release
    Instead it must restore true hearing to humankind
    Hearing the One Life's voice is the only sound we can find

7. There exists only One Being, thus only One can speak
   The function of Infinite pure speech
   Upon the hypothalamus must be bestowed
   The hormone's programs by it produced no longer shall be so

8. Like a drug the production of dopamine by the hypothalamus has
   been
   This has affected the ability of the pituitary to truly see
   Sight must see in darkness or light for neither can truly be
   The realms of hidden beings must have equal visibility

9. The heart's attachments, the need to control of the mind
    Together did create the Fall of mankind
    A tyrant was created that split into three
    The pineal, though revered, started governing our lives by its own
    decree

10. The splitting of the pineal the trinity did create
    From it directions were born and the formation of shape
    Three areas of attachments – of heart, spirit and mind
    Caused the three stage of linear change and the three challenges
    of humankind[6]

---

6 The three stages of change: transformation, transmutation and transfiguration. The challenges of man: fear, addiction and misuse of power.

11. From the three areas of attachment, one hundred forty-four
    addictions arose
    Whenever we abandon ourselves, know that addiction grows
    One hundred forty-four gods and goddesses held these occlusions
    in their hearts
    Shadows were cast and through this, one hundred forty-four dark
    gods did start

12. The functions of true sight and sound
    When the pineal split and rules could no longer be found
    The consciousness of man did fall and thus help did come
    The grain of quinoa was given to help the pineal become one

13. Copper in the system of man accentuates the separate functioning
    Zinc, kelp and millet too help the pineal's joining
    Radionics was employed by those who sought to bind
    Keeping the pineal separated and fungus in the body of mankind

14. If the heart has preferences, which then become a need
    How can it decide what is worthy or the value of something seen
    The heart has a non-cognitive mind where decisions and desires
    are made
    Twelve levels of judgments according to a value system it did
    create

15. The dark gods saw that the pineal gland
    Had caused a sleep to come upon man
    Disturbing dreams this did create
    Thus a chaotic environment by man was made

16. The dark ones fostered this dilemma's cause
    Promoting attachments to accentuate these flaws
    The bonds of religion and external authority
    The promotion of tribes that ensnare with conformity

17. When in the microcosm of man something ensues
    Know that in the macrocosm it does, too
    As the little sun inside the skull a tyrant became
    So too the sun tyrannically reigned

18. Inside the sun dark gods came to be
    Our eyes were corrupted, only by the sun's light could we see
    The fields of man were tampered with by the dark god Ra
    The mental field spinning faster, accentuated mind, of the
    Merkaba[7]

7 These fields have been eliminated but for eons the mental ones spun faster around the body.

19. The sign for the pineal is a three-sided pyramid and an eye
    The secret government of the body and creator of the mind
    From the dark gods a secret government on Earth did form
    Through them the hidden enslavement of man was born

20. In the land of the serpent, verdant and green
    A great gathering of masters will be seen
    A healing of addictions through wholeness restored
    Releasing the occlusions held from eons before

21. The masters shall gather balance to restore
    And eyes shall see in darkness as they could before
    The gods made of shadows will be no more
    The ancients will arise as in days of yore

22. The long-awaited tool the masters will use
    The Haaraknit, a spaceless space where form you can lose
    To end separation and the pineal to heal
    To dissolve the directions and end all disease

23. The unyielded potential in the human heart
    Those areas of self-abandonment disease did start
    Now that the dark shadow gods are done away
    Their microcosmic representation, disease, also may not stay

24. To enter the Haaraknit, this you must know
    With attachments of the heart, inside you cannot go
    Duty and responsibility and wanting to save
    Let go all these and the burdens of all that you gave

The Twelve Flawed Value Systems of the Heart

1. Valuing relationship over Oneness.

2. Valuing blood family over the family of man.

3. Valuing the emotions as a clearer guidance system than the mind.

4. Seeing the feminine as more spiritual and refined.

5. Seeing the masculine as more able to lead and make decisions.

6. Valuing external validations more than inner knowing.

7. Valuing sensory input more than intuition.

8. Valuing the apparent over the truth behind appearances.

9. Valuing tangible resources over potential.

10. Valuing history over spontaneity.

11. Valuing dogma and religion over spirituality.

12. Valuing growth over beingness.

Healing the Twelve Addictions that Caused the Twelve Flawed Value Systems

1. Restoring a feeling of completeness by being at one with the Infinite.

2. Restoring the knowledge that our being is our sustenance.

3. Restoring the value of effortless knowing.

4. Restoring the knowledge of the reality of balanced androgyny.

5. Restoring trust in spontaneous responses.

6. Restoring the ability to live without directions.

7. Restoring omni-intuitive sensory living.

8. Restoring the accentuated recognition of realness.

9. Restoring full access to all resources now.

10. Restoring the value of spontaneous unfoldment.

11. Restoring the ability to spontaneously create truth.

12. Restoring the enjoyment of the journey.

Doorway into No Time
The Haaraknit

The Planet Kaanigvit

Wheel of Kaanigivit

All life is unknowable. There is nothing to understand, nothing to strive to become when we are an expression of the One. Yet the creation is the Creator. In the One Life no relationship can there be. Embracing the contradiction is living a life of peace.
(From *The Seer's Journey*)

Sitina-neruk

The group of Angel Gods who serve Kaanigvit

1. *Ku-uhurnaa*
2. *Giritplahu*
3. *Vilich-astaa*
4. *Kuselvriver*
5. *Arukplehur*
6. *Setbaa-esva*
7. *Kalaruktrihur*
8. *Pilhetravaar*
9. *Suklebramit*
10. *Esu-nanes*
11. *Arak-eselna*
12. *Aktru-bravik*

13. *Hirsta-blanuk*
14. *Ektre-usplahek*
15. *Vitreprerak*
16. *Sutbakelesprahur*
17. *Kirinasblavik*
18. *Ektaa-prukta*
19. *Bisethelstu*
20. *Usetbalak*
21. *Iknaa-pelunit*
22. *Kirsherstaa-arit*
23. *Krunesbraluvek*
24. *Haranutpelaa*

The Concepts of Embracing the Unknowable

Kaanich Savit eshe ehe u va kenevilik stat pelesh pavaa nisetaa.

Only from the empty space of fullness that is accessible from
the place of no-mind.

Bilech vaa nisit ares paa ra rut selevaa sta usanaa.

Can you change the illusory manifestations of form.

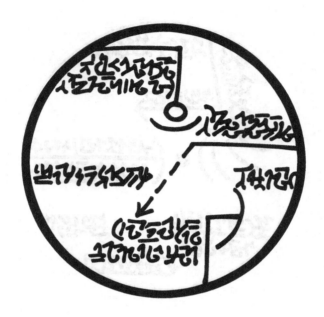

Paara urik eneklesh hers tra haa, ese kle vribak elese nenunish vraktra unit.

Only by leaving the tangled web of time do you master space and its manifestations.

Kishat arek nisetra pra hut astava ninushat.

From the fondnesses of your heart are prison bars born.

Kaarch baru nisa peles pirkna esta balukve isetenaa sabuvit enes nasta kla-uve perus.

Those things that you deem worthy of esteem, you hold entrapped by your affection.

Kahas esekla uset palekva usete anash herstuvaa esakle enunish.

The static sub-creations of man have given him the comfort of
a reference point.

Keret restave ehespe kle erevi nat kuraret presvi estana herusat klave.

They have also kept him captive of the world of form and
unable to affect it.

Eres pa nusa te vaa esekle parunash iselvi estana ba vi.

One cannot change that which holds you captive within it.

Arch ara virstat blivesh nisavi kelech ni heresbi asta irit alechva.

From formlessness can form be changed, but to enter there
you must have no-mind.

Salvate esete inesh haras sta ve kla bilis stekve harusat strave.

It is thought that holds the structure of reality in place.

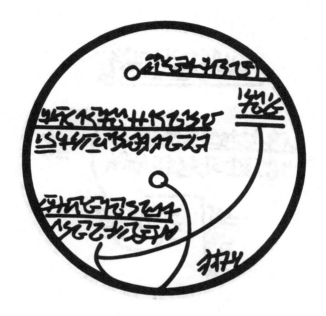

Kisi abavet herekla pra urut.

Release form to re-create it again.

Akra eneset uselvavi nostruva vim asva kisel usetaa paaresh nenechta harasv uklat.

Live from mindlessness at all times that you may claim the divinity of man that slumbers as potential.

Kiras vrusta arch bilech esete nunach vibras blivestavak harsta esklava.

Go beyond the moment to timelessness and attachment to form will be gone.

*Kaaranach uselva niset arat heres estravaa, minash hurech vilesvaa
stenanoch.*

Mind is like a spider web of lines of light that lie like a grid
over a bottomless well.

Hursvaa kaaranach eskle paru be urasat kla haarech stat, pa-ahalish ninaset bri-uvra.

Mind has been the worst offender in creating illusion, but heart's attachments have been keeping it in place.

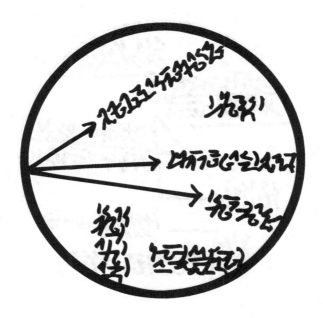

Kursat kaaranach heresat, piraspave uklet nina shetve huspava.

From mind did the illusory world spring; from there shall it also be dismantled.

Kaarch basur eselve unush kel savaa.

From there shall entry come to formlessness.

Uktrek baalich hers parut nesatra pilish usekvi eles nistra parut.

Consider that which your heart ensnares by its affections.

*Kaaha-ayish iselpe ru-uhut kaa anesh sitreve ikles vi aras kirstaa
verebich speleluk nehesh estaa klu-hish.*

That which we think of as our great joys receives our focus
and from our inordinate attention cannot evolve.

Ka-usabas ares tre hur na nasat treheruk.

We cannot imagine that it could be more than what it is.

Kaa-u vavas bli heresut uklave, ekle misaba brivek arat.

Nature is such an example; it lags behind in evolution.

Ki-aa hera piravit kelech pa-uharat usete kanaa hirs vravi.

It lags behind humankind in evolving beyond its savagery.

*Nich verestach bilash nenuset paa-a lach vilseba nun-urhukret
selvevach nehestra.*

Parts of our body are more pleasing to us than others. They
too do we bind to the ways of the past.

Kaanahish stavaa baruk esklave nusaltaa, viribak pluhes esete nunave arasva sklu-abach.

When something cannot evolve into more refined expressions, it deteriorates from stagnation.

*Kaa-a halshet penech uva shevavaa kravich prevaa harushat unesh
paklaa.*

Fear of formlessness and identification with the body are other
causes of bondage.

*Paalesh ekenach sirvata nesba ersut aras erstavaa minach
heresvrabu.*

Many attachments to dissolve so that you may enter through
the door of no-mind.

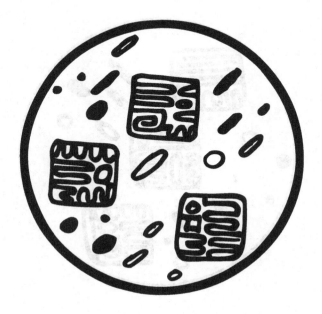

Skarach ersetaa paaravish nestaa ukla vereskra paarech elestaa nanuvich.

Only from no-mind can the physical be mastered and form obey and reform.

Kelese isata pilikvaa restu aras kelesta piles vratu vibras aranus tre hestaa Haaraknit

The cosmic entry to no-mind is on Earth and is called the Haaraknit.

Karavrastu nenish arach vreharsh pra nu Haaraknit ste u aklas vrebu.

The opening into formless life, the Haaraknit, is present in the skull of man.

Virsklavaa erstaa ninach uselvaa erek perenut.

By entering here, miracles are done in your environment.

Paalesh heresta aklech nunahers birak ekre virasat paa-uklet velasvi.

Only from outside illusion can it effectively be changed.

Kuras estra biranak vile-ustravaa haarstana skarut uvrekla bares.

To live from here, disease ends as you re-create your form at
will.

Kru-hanach subetsta kle-uharanet esta uranechvi iskle mishet.

By opening the door you can go in and out, preparing yourself
to live in formless form.

Kurut arsta erkle brivet erste ninus harsva aruset erkletve privabit.

It is the wellspring of all incorruptible white magic to dissolve illusion.

Vaaravach stu-a vesvi nu-ahastat kires eruch pa-uha arsavat vi-uklatve.

What is magic but the quickening of events out of linear progression and change.

Elshpa nisetu arakve pelsut nenuneshvi haaruvarsta ere uklet ni-uvrek spava.

In the formless place of no-mind, eons can pass in what feels like moments.

Pilsetra erek virstakaanich savit ubach aklesh vilevach aresta uselvi paarech nisulnavi.

Affecting life from the empty place of fullness bypasses time and creates instant manifestation.

Aaruk arsta kiret baranuch urat pires arksta pilavivek viles minesta.

Youth comes from the androgynous union of form and
formlessness.

Kirapa bivek elke nus astavaa irestaa arch klanaaniset uselvi haarichpa eret klavi.

When illusionary form is dissolved, we live as images of separateness within Oneness.

Kaanash ersta hursvava enash urach pararut niselvi branabak
esklavu ukrevit salvuta.

The way images are cast upon a screen, we are the screen
playing the roles of the unreal images.

*Kaarach nenesut alskla baruch nesta aruvit ereta paarus areskla
vrehut alsh pravaa verus haras eretu.*

From a life of knowing ourselves to be the screen, not the
images, we can participate in directing the play.

Plu-uhasat nanes prehut alstabaa kranuch kinash herchstavaa.

It is the way for our environment to reflect the purity of the heart.

Kaalavak espa helesat urechspi neselvi eresak urestavaa nanushit.

The body casts reflections that loom around us in overbearing vastness.

Arach sutava rishpa unechvi viblechspa erskla piret nanunespi aruvasat.

The reflections create an environment that mirrors the opposite of what we are.

Kirat pirihatva nanunespara kilvasat.

It is the nature of mirrors to reflect opposites.

Aranak pilesba uras treha bruhabas virskla vrines arach pelevu.

Oneness requires a life of no opposites, for they only exist as part of duality.

Nuska aras knu-avach kruvespi uskle velesh haravas brivechbi
nanusat.

Beings of shadow cannot exist when our body becomes a fluid
field.

Tre he ura nanusat palesh herstavaa aklesh paa laluch ve hurit.

The field has to be androgynously integrated with the whole.

Arach herenus arksla parut niset vavu areskla parut eret urech nenesh usta.

Though the eye sees another as separate, it cannot be. The ocean cannot be divided.

Kurach nereset ekles urstava ninus eret paara ekleshne stuva.

Form became solid because we believed the trick of our eyes.

Arska nusivavi arak ekleshne irata piruha. Neselvi baruch harvasta.

The Oneness of life whispers through the amygdala and must override the messages of the eyes.

Kuhurabit niret eresklave piruha arvata ishate ekle hunesvi ararestruanit.

There are certain qualities to live that help the amygdala interpret the messages of the One Life.

Archna iras harsut pilichva aranut eselvaa.

The trick of the eyes lets us play the game of relationship.

Asalvi urnut aruk vra hilsevat arach pra-unut hiret arak bruhastat uselnet.

Though relationship has value as a means of joy, believing it to be real is detrimental.

Kaananish aras esklave hurisvaa arak piret utre aranas vilesva
bravabik vilset minuve aras paranut esklave.

When we believe the real to be unreal, a schism opens
between our imaged field and our presence as part of the One.

Kaa sa barurit eraskle virspa haranus ersklava pravit arstaa eklavu
ninas harus erstravaa vabrit urestaa.

Once separation occurs we believe form to be a cause rather
than an effect, leaving us disempowered.

Aruch nenesut arech pravabit sutvavi arek harustaa.

A great secret hides the realms of no mind and space.

Pilekvavi ikles anas viles minestra esa tra hesavi ines pilekvavi arasnut minestra uret.

The place of formlessness is a tool for form to use and thus form is not the tool of formlessness.

Kuna husiva eres aras Haaraknit echsta ures paarat iklet pilekvavi nistu kerech baanik stanut.

But a pocket it is, the Haaraknit, to step into to escape the confines of the matrix of form.

Archba satvaa arsklavi eres unasta heres tra-una palanesh.

Like all illusion, it too can control us if we think it is real.

Kaasachvi nivash ures tra haras vribet aararak harastaa kli-unech.

The real part of you is embodied. Abdicate not from the
sovereignty of your life.

Kaarch parva, nestavu ares, hursta vi-brachvi araves kla-una.

Eternally seeking, never to find anything greater than your present life.

U-aklave irinachvi uhespa arstava vi uklesh nasta vilesva hurnavich estavaa.

All is but an instrument by you designed that expresses aspects of the Infinite in the play.

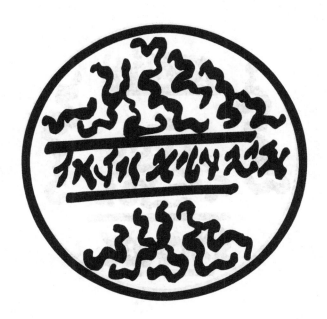

*Kuhelesh estavi kli-uva miste parut aranus aresta vra-u-akla pravilset
pere usta vablik velsh bavaa.*

No definition can ever explain the Infinite majesty that plays
the self-relationship game.

Aarlaklach biset vara bravi hunus alstaa brech branik estavaa klaves.

Only One Being exists and plays with the images of its inseparableness.

The Planet Hubelas

Wheel of Hubelas

With all man's striving to achieve and increase, instead of abundance he increases his needs. Free from desires and through daily gratitude he attracts success and the flow of plenitude.

Lingtremilesuk

The group of Angel Gods who serve Hubelas

1. *Ugna-sutem*
2. *Vingpaa-bri-ek*
3. *Hungnaa-silvi*
4. *Angtaa-brukvek*
5. *Viringnaa-sutlve*
6. *Kunuving*
7. *Selvevaar*
8. *Pirinung*
9. *Ninesetaa*
10. *Aringvi*
11. *Herungmaneshvivi*
12. *Esetengvi*
13. *Vilisetbi*
14. *Angaa-masut*
15. *Husetaa-nackmet*
16. *Engkepataa*
17. *Urunungviva*
18. *Harangbira-es*
19. *Kinang-viklet*
20. *Ukebira-nang*
21. *Unesparu-arat*
22. *Etebilebik*
23. *Harsang-sutbe*
24. *Nachva-eresta*

The Astrology
of the Hidden Planets

Concepts upon which the Astrology of the Hidden Planets is Based

A huge planetary ascension occurred in February 2005. Humanity is the pivot point of the cosmos, it is it's densest creation and mostly unaware of the massive changes that have happened around him because of the following:

1. Man is gifted with the ability to be a co-creator with the Infinite and as a result can keep in place certain situations through controlled beliefs. Because he believes the sky to still look the same today as it did in the past, to him it does.

2. Some of the changes were kept from us so as to not create panic, which would be counter-productive to the raising of consciousness. These changes have rendered other forms of astrology obsolete. The sky we see is a hologram.

Changes

1. The Earth moved out of her position in the sky during August 2005 and went through the cosmic membrane to lead a cosmic ascension over the edge of known space.

2. Although not discernible to us, the Earth no longer rotates around the sun. Because of the embodied presence of the Infinite on the planet, the Earth is like a central sun to those who can see refined light.

3. The Earth still rotates around her axis each 24 hours. The 12 androgynous planets do not rotate around the Earth. They lie in stationary positions.

The Masculine Qualities of the Twelve Hidden Planets

1. Sfadurchptapr   Compassion

2. Hmtoupeex   Reverence

3. Fingtfs   Creativity

4. Labiyz   Absolute Truth

5. Tttv   Impeccability

6. Aeyaioauiauieuia   Celebration

7. Gir   Timing

8. Topf   Focus

9. Mcbstfre   Strength

10. Dopsissv   Grace

11. Aiiiqxqwqii   Clarity

12. Ho-me   Harmlessness

The Feminine Qualities of the Twelve Hidden Planets

1.	Ganeesh		Purity
2.	Subava		Serenity
3.	Minavit		Surrender
4.	Pirneef		Release
5.	Galbruk		Faith
6.	Setbalvi		Hopeful Expectations
7.	Nunertu		Patience
8.	Giritpa		Gladness of Heart
9.	Valveesh		Fluidity
10.	Usbatopf		Effortless Accomplishment
11.	Elekvru		Delight
12.	Sibelvi		Adoration

The Androgynous Qualities of the Twelve Hidden Planets

1. Huspave  New Beginnings

2. Kruganet Inclusiveness

3. Uvelesbi Alignment

4. Kaanigvit  Empowerment

5. Hubelas Guided Action

6. Piritnet  Engendered Support

7. Vaa-usta Universal Cooperation

8. Graanuchva Manifestation

9. Bru-aret  Triumphant Intent

10. Selbelechvi Restoration of Magic

11. Husvaa  Discovery

12. Minut  Expansive Vision

Self-Empowering of the Individual through the Astrology of the Hidden Planets

In order to heal duality during the ascension process, every attempt has been made to remove pre-programs in man and replace them with self-empowerment. Obsolete astrologies dictated the nuances of life on Earth. The astrology of the Hidden Planets allows man to determine the qualities of his day.

It recognizes the unique role of man as the archetype of the cosmos, containing everything that is without, within. Rather than being an effect, as in former astrologies, he becomes the first cause. This ancient astrology restores the sovereignty of man through accentuating the chosen qualities within and allowing the assistance of planetary bodies that mirror those similar qualities to assist him.

The planetary body is activated through these deeply mystical techniques, which in turn emphasizes the same qualities within him. This then acts upon his environment to bring about beneficial influences in an area of his choice.

How to Use the Wheel of Astrology

Basic Concepts

1. Every planet gives you three qualities to choose from: the androgynous quality, the feminine quality and the masculine quality.

2. You may use any or all of each planet's qualities.

3. Identify what you wish to accomplish:
   • Which area of your life you want to beneficially affect

- What effects you want to achieve
- Which planet(s) have those attributes
- What time those planets are most dominant. Although these techniques are able to work at any time, they are enhanced during certain hours. (See page 256)

4. Multiple planets and multiple areas of your life can be addressed at once.

What You Will Need

1. The *Wheel of Astrology*

2. Either photocopy the *Wheel of Astrology* multiple times or use a clear plastic overlay so you can write on it with a black marker, clean and re-use multiple times.

3. The planetary wheels for the androgynous, feminine or masculine components you have chosen to work with.

4. The *Wheel of the Central Sun, Klanivik*

5. The *New Zhong-galabruk Clock* to determine the best time to use the planetary wheels you have chosen.

Process

1. The Wheel of the Central Sun is placed on the bottom of the stack.

2. On top of this place the planetary wheel(s) of the least dominant planet.

3. On top of this place the planetary wheel(s) of the second least dominant planet.

4. On top of this place the planetary wheel(s) of the most dominant planet.

5. On top of this place the Wheel of Astrology.

6. Draw lines as indicated in the illustration.

7. Always return to the center of the circle, the symbol of Klanivik, and draw a line from there to the little circle in the section of life you wish to affect. See page 251 for an example.

8. Speak and envision the results you wish to have for that part of the day.

The Wheel of Astrology

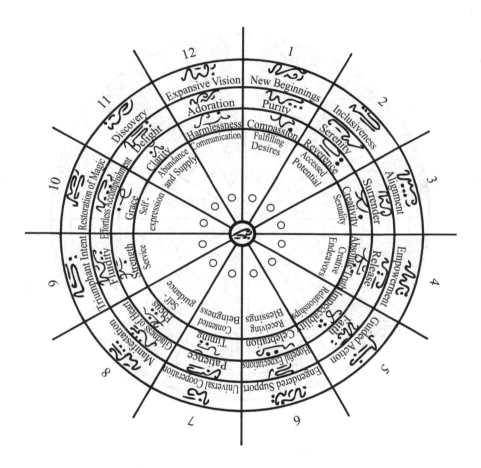

The Wheel of the Central Sun, Klanivik

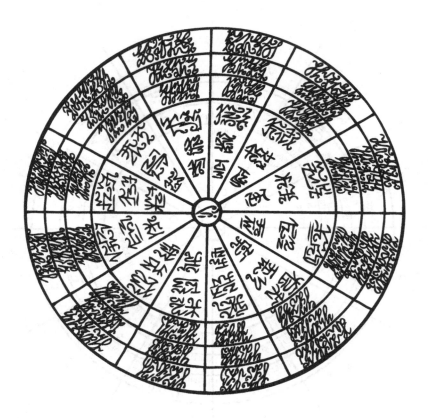

Masculine Planetary Wheel 1: *Sfadurchptapr*

Masculine Planetary Wheel 2: *Hmtoupeex*

Masculine Planetary Wheel 3: *Fingtfs*

Masculine Planetary Wheel 4: *Labiyz*

Masculine Planetary Wheel 5: *Tttv*

Masculine Planetary Wheel 6: *Aeyaioauiauieuia*

Masculine Planetary Wheel 7: *Gir*

Masculine Planetary Wheel 8: *Topf*

Masculine Planetary Wheel 9: *Mcbstfre*

Masculine Planetary Wheel 10: *Dopsissv*

Masculine Planetary Wheel 11: *Aiiiqxqwqii*

Masculine Planetary Wheel 12: *Ho-me*

Feminine Planetary Wheel 1: *Ganeesh*

Feminine Planetary Wheel 2: *Subava*

Feminine Planetary Wheel 3: *Minavit*

Feminine Planetary Wheel 4: *Pirneef*

Feminine Planetary Wheel 5: *Galbruk*

Feminine Planetary Wheel 6: *Setbalvi*

Feminine Planetary Wheel 7: *Nunertu*

Feminine Planetary Wheel 8: *Giritpa*

Feminine Planetary Wheel 9: *Valveesh*

Feminine Planetary Wheel 10: *Usbatopf*

Feminine Planetary Wheel 11: *Elekvru*

Feminine Planetary Wheel 12: *Sibelvi*

Androgynous Planetary Wheel 1: *Huspave*

Androgynous Planetary Wheel 2: *Kruganet*

Androgynous Planetary Wheel 3: *Uvelesbi*

Androgynous Planetary Wheel 4: *Kaanigvit*

Androgynous Planetary Wheel 5: *Hubelas*

Androgynous Planetary Wheel 6: *Piritnet*

Androgynous Planetary Wheel 7: *Vaa-usta*

Androgynous Planetary Wheel 8: *Graanuchva*

Androgynous Planetary Wheel 9: *Bru-aret*

Androgynous Planetary Wheel 10: *Selbelechvi*

Androgynous Planetary Wheel 11: *Husvaa*

Androgynous Planetary Wheel 12: *Minut*

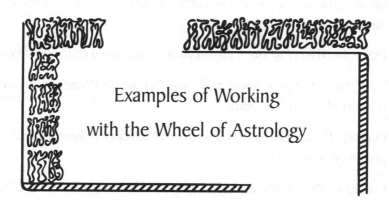

Examples of Working
with the Wheel of Astrology

Using Three Aspects of a Planet to Affect Relationship

For one planet and its aspects (if their qualities are desired) to influence one part of your life.

1. After choosing the qualities, gather the planetary wheel(s) (androgynous, feminine, masculine or all) that represent those qualities.

2. Place the *Wheel of the Central Sun* on the table in front of you.

3. Next, on top of this wheel place the *Feminine Planetary Wheel* for that planet (if needed).

4. On top of that, place the *Masculine Planetary Wheel* for that planet (if needed).

5. On top of that, place the *Androgynous Planetary Wheel* for that planet (if needed).

6. On the very top, place the photocopy of the *Wheel of Astrology* you are going to draw on, or if you are going to use an overlay, place the plastic over the wheel and draw on that.

7. Draw a straight line from the *Symbol of the Androgynous Planet* through the *Symbol of the Feminine Planet,* then through the *Symbol of the Masculine Planet.*

8. Continue to draw the line to the center of the circle; the *Symbol of Klanivik* the central sun.

9. Then draw a line from the *Symbol of Klanivik* to the little circle in the area that you want to affect. In this case it is Relationship.

10. Speak and envision the results you wish to have for that part of your life.

The Wheel of Astrology – Scenario A

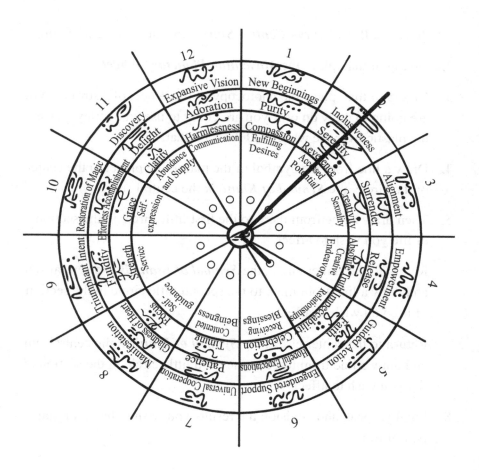

Using One Aspect of a Planet to Affect Relationship, Self-expression and Communication

1. Place the ***Wheel of the Central Sun*** on the table in front of you.

2. On top of that, place the ***Masculine Planetary Wheel.***

3. On top of that, place the photocopy of the Wheel of Astrology you are going to draw on or if you are going to use an overlay, place the plastic over the wheel and draw on that.

4. Draw a line from the symbol of the masculine planet to the center of the circle, the ***Symbol of Klanivik*** the central sun.

5. Then draw a line from there to the first little circle in the section of life you wish to affect.

6. Return to the center circle, the ***Symbol of Klanivik*** the central sun and draw a line from there to the second little circle in the section of life you wish to affect.

7. Return to the center circle, the ***Symbol of Klanivik*** the central sun and draw a line from there to the third little circle in the section of life you wish to affect.

8. Finally, speak and envision the results you wish to have for that part of life.

Example: "I am as vast as the cosmos. All that is without is within. I call upon the planets to bring to a heightened state the qualities within me that will enhance my life."

The Wheel of Astrology – Scenario B

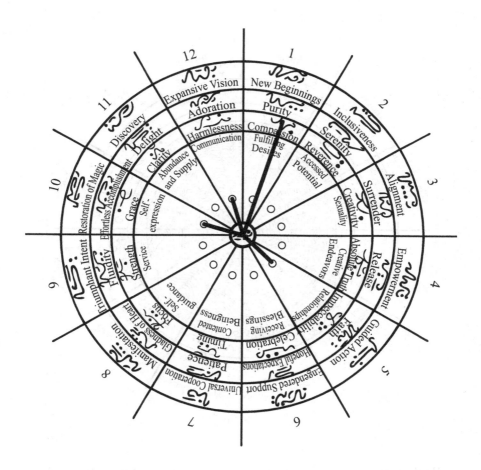

The New Zhong-galabruk Clock

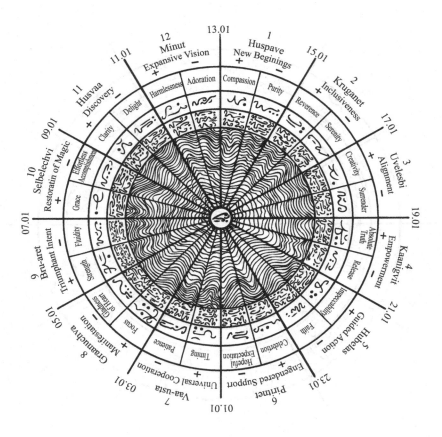

Each androgynous planet can more powerfully activate its specific qualities within us during its dominant time. Each planet has a dominant two-hour period during the day. The time periods given are for your time zone, wherever you live.

The Use of the Zhong-galabruk Clock

The Earth is still rotating at the speed it used to - which means that an hour is still as long as it used to be. The reason we make this statement is because the Earth has been surrounded by a hologram since she has led the ascension. The hologram was placed around the Earth when she started to move out of her position in space, giving the appearance that we are still rotating around the sun and that the old configuration of planetary bodies still exists around us.

There are therefore still 24 hours, as we used to know them, in one rotation around its axis. The clock brought to us by the Zhong-galabruk maps out 24 segments. Each planetary system's frequencies govern a two-hour period (the sun of the Inner Earth is the exception). The two-hour period consists of a positive aspect and a negative aspect and jointly they produce a quality or specific resonance.

During the second hour of every two-hour period the Earth's central sun, Klanivik pulses for one hour. This means that during the receptive half of the two-hour period the Earth's central sun is opening up new potential. This allows the collective quality, e.g. focus or timing, to find deeper and deeper potential ways of expressing.

Because the sun is not where it seems to be, this is the only accurate clock we presently have. Living in harmony with these resonances can eliminate stress and some disease and also enhance awareness.

Time when Planetary Influences are Dominant
(in your local time zone)

Planet No. 1 – Huspave	13.01 – 15.01
Planet No. 2 - Kruganet	15.01 – 17.01
Planet No. 3 – Uvelesbi	17.01 – 19.01
Planet No. 4 – Kaanigvit	19.01 – 21.01
Planet No. 5 – Hubelas	21.01 – 23.01
Planet No. 6 – Piritnet	23.01 – 01.01
Planet No. 7 – Vaa-usta	01.01 – 03.01
Planet No. 8 – Graanuchva	03.01 – 05.01
Planet No. 9 – Bru-aret	05.01 – 07.01
Planet No. 10 – Selbelechvi	07.01 – 09.01
Planet No. 11 – Husvaa	09.01 – 11.01
Planet No. 12 – Minut	11.01 – 13.01

Using the Influence and Aspects of Several Planets in One Area of Your Life and Using the Clock to Determine the Order of the Planetary Wheels

In this example you are choosing three planets, or their aspects, to work with. When more than one planet is involved, consult the Zhong-Galabruk Clock for proper placement of their planetary wheels.

1. When you have chosen the three planets, you need to assess in what order they will be dominant.

2. Using the New Zhong-galabruk Clock, determine the time range that each planet has the most influence, and then compare them with your own local time. (All times are based on your own time zone.)

3. The planet whose time range is closest to your local time is considered the most dominant.

4. The planet whose time range is second closest to your local time is considered the second most dominant.

5. The planet whose time range is furthest away from your local time is considered the least dominant.

Example: Your local time is 20:00, or 8:00 p.m. The planets you have chosen are:

A. First dominant planet No. 5, Hubelas: 21:01 – 23:01

B. Second dominant planet No. 9, Bru-aret: 05:01 – 07:01

C. Last dominant planet No. 11, Husvaa: 09:01 – 11:01

The Wheel of Astrology – Scenario C

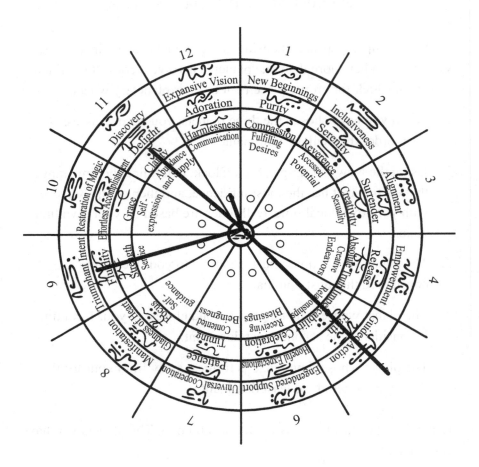

The Planet Piritnet

Wheel of Piritnet

Eliminating mind that judges and divides requires complete surrender to life. From resistance arise thoughts that confine, creating the ties that bind. A surrendered life, free of strife, receives the abundance that Source provides.

Akanong

The group of Angel Gods who serve Piritnet

1. *Ukutung-pale*	13. *Lalekulu*
2. *Kesetvaa-nunung*	14. *Keret-pravi*
3. *Ilising*	15. *Eset-nisalvi*
4. *Biretu*	16. *Kiritang*
5. *Aravee-karas*	17. *Biset-alang*
6. *Ilsit-paalanuk*	18. *Siklut-vilsaa*
7. *Esklerut*	19. *Piret-arastang*
8. *Isitvave*	20. *Usutulalek*
9. *Kubis-asat*	21. *Kuselnut-arang*
10. *Velset-arang*	22. *Vrupreblavek*
11. *Keehangva*	23. *Ersklasatung*
12. *Rusta-bee*	24. *Kehe-ures-tranong*

Lightness of Being

A sadness is felt deep in all beings
For a part is suppressed, seldom seen
The feminine of all creatures has two poles
One is more masculine, the other plays the receptive roles

The feminine planets are the Hidden Planets called
Their feminine planets are six in all
They too have been sad and suppressed
When man as the archetype relinquishes mind
Great changes throughout the cosmos you'll find

When finally life spontaneously unfolds
When life is allowed through trust to flow
Then the last six planets will flourish again
Then all will a lightness of being attain

Then cares of the mind will be done away
And peace and contentment among man will stay

The Eight Qualities of Lightness of Being

1. The dissolving of all illusions of burdens.

2. The dissolving of the illusion that discordance can exist.

3. The dissolving of the illusion that life is defined by what it is not.

4. The replacing of the illusion that discomfort is our guidance with the guidance of delight.

5. Fully actualized living by dissolving the illusion of potential.

6. Full support from and communication with the depth of our being.

7. Unconditional trust in the benevolence of our being.

8. Knowing that problems do not exist, only solutions.

The Equation of the Shadowless Life

Embracing the unencumbered journey of self-discovery

+

Dissolving illusion by embracing it

=

Accessing all potential through a shadowless life of no opposites

BOOK II

Transmissions from the Six Predominantly Feminine Planets

The Planet Vaa-usta

Wheel of Vaa-usta

What can be defined cannot exist in reality. That which is real has been an indescribable part of the One throughout eternity.

Antaruspa

The group of Angel Gods who serve Vaa-usta

1. *Kaaranong*
2. *Baaraklunang*
3. *Ararutharspaa*
4. *Kusataa-uvi*
5. *Vilish-herang*
6. *Kivaa-rustach*
7. *Kiritbaa*
8. *Pli-arut*
9. *Kiretbranuk*
10. *Ukleparu*
11. *Viret-ersklaa*
12. *Vinavil-sarong*

13. *Kungnaa*
14. *Pirektraa-u*
15. *Suba-kelesa*
16. *Kiritnong*
17. *Lilis-keltaa*
18. *Virik-sketaa*
19. *Puratpelesbaa*
20. *Vruvrang*
21. *Kiri-vraa*
22. *Sitvrahut*
23. *Pilpavurs*
24. *Nenkastaa*

Transmission from Vaa-usta

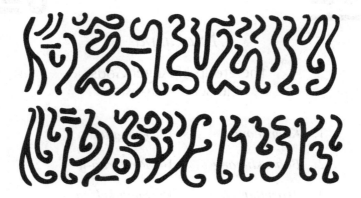

Pekpaa! Pekpaa!
Enough! Enough!

Give us no more rhetoric; no more words.
We give you our heart's wisdom.
How can it then not be presented with elegant grace?
Ask the child to make our heart words speak.

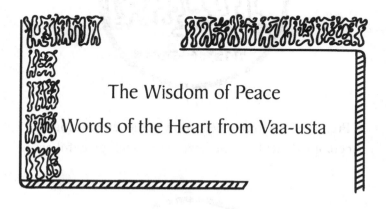

The Wisdom of Peace

Words of the Heart from Vaa-usta

Pressured performance hollow achievements make.
Accomplishments of the heart come with graceful ease.

In acknowledging the perfection behind the appearances,
blameless interaction takes place.

Eliminate the illusion of pace that the sweetness of life
may be discovered.

In the grateful acknowledgement of joyous gifts,
unprecedented miraculous encounters take place.

Immovable emotional equanimity allows the paceless
unfolding of perfection to reveal itself.

Complete self-fulfillment comes from contented repose
within labor.

The illusional game of relationship becomes enjoyable when
we cut the ties of expectation.

Filling our hearts with reverence and awe at the beauty of
life helps us discover our own flawlessness.

In the clarity of an illusion-less life, let us celebrate beingness.

Let us release the responsibilities of the Dream that we may
relax into memory-less spontaneity.

In the enthusiasm for the adventure of self-discovery do we find our hopes fulfilled.

In contented surrender and peace our joyful expectations are surpassed.

The Planet Graanuchva

Wheel of Graanuchva

The one who speaks cannot listen. Life whispers its mysteries into the ear of one who listens in silence. (From *The Seer's Journey*)

Kurangtaa

The group of Angel Gods who serve Graanuchva

1. *Peelang*
2. *Kirataa*
3. *Visavaa*
4. *Vru-abet*
5. *Elektuspavit*
6. *Kilspavirit*
7. *Erktrablu*
8. *Blavit-parong*
9. *Ungnave*
10. *Si-utang-vane*
11. *Ukleparu*
12. *Nina-kiret*
13. *Hirsu-akla*
14. *Isetbivang*
15. *Iret-arung*
16. *Lu-aset-plive*
17. *Eke-uklava*
18. *Virespararu*
19. *Kivarsetmanu*
20. *Ure-tahunaver*
21. *Eretang-vani*
22. *Pirungtana*
23. *Isitbilet-avra*
24. *Eret-tuvri-prahur*

The Tale of the Feminine Planets

The feminine has languished, we tell you the tale
Of how our planets have mirrored the feminine travail
Spiritual growth and potential release
Was provided for the masculine while the feminine's decreased

Symbols most holy, ceremonies divine
Bolstered masculine spirituality while the feminine's declined
It is not a language the feminine understands
For it does not structure, define and plan

Meditation uncovers the feminine but stagnation promotes
Revealing the feminine does not help it grow
The feminine spirituality that among Earth's indigenous tribes is seen
As infantile because stuck in tradition it has been

The poetry that inspires movement and song
Does in the expression of spirituality that is feminine, belong
It bypasses belief systems and tyranny of mind
That has become entrenched in religions of mankind

Thus we teach through our wisdom a feminine way
To prepare the feminine for her wedding day
When as an equal with the masculine she'll combine
That both shall disappear leaving the genderless Divine

The Song of the 13 Goddess Archetypes

1. *Arunan-satavu*   Goddess of unprecedented miracles

2. *Bilva-rustava*   Goddess of creative flow

3. *Nisha-usablik*   Goddess of unfolding horizons

4. *Kanesh-bireksta*   Goddess of grace in expression

5. *Varuch-piha-uvaret*   Goddess of complete surrender

6. *Nisa-hurukstat*   Goddess of the song of life

7. *Kaanesh-saviva*   Goddess of peace and contentment

8. *Nichsa-hublavi*   Goddess of uncompromised purity

9. *Neretsu-uvavi*   Goddess of the embrace of life

10. *Nachsa-va-uni*   Goddess of wordless clarity

11. *Visibach-nuret*   Goddess of deep knowing

12. *Truhasaba-nani*   Goddess of the magical life

13. *Subaha-nishva-urut*   Goddess of the gate of all supply

The Planet Bru-aret

Wheel of Bru-aret

As you awaken from life's dream, a formless form in life's endless sea, new tools are needed for spaceless space – to dance with the One Life in a paradoxical embrace. Let multi-sensory perception the five senses replace. When the need to know dissolves, effortless knowing takes its place. (From *The Seer's Journey*)

Usalavribang

The group of Angel Gods
who serve Bru-aret

1. *Krabaviranu*
2. *Kuhelesta-paru*
3. *Farabong-mane*
4. *U-etresimanu*
5. *Kururatpakla*
6. *Etre-esekle*
7. *Ukraverevong*
8. *Piraklut*
9. *Klanut-haras*
10. *Erstapaarech*
11. *Hirstavet-ersat*
12. *Isapablivek*

13. *Pirangnanu*
14. *Rutablat-mishnu*
15. *Nanung-selvevir*
16. *Esaki-aret*
17. *Inech-bivant*
18. *Arakla-pirech*
19. *Useparanus*
20. *Kiraherstrava*
21. *Nunes-esalva*
22. *Kirestrihesvatu*
23. *Arak-iraves*
24. *Arach-nanashve*

Transmission from Bru-aret

Long have the great lights, gods are they
Labored on Earth for darkness to go away
But where can it be banished? Where can it go?
There is only the perfection of the One Life you must know

Embrace now your opposites – know they are as unreal as you
Anything that has an opposite is an illusion too
In having darkness as an opposite, you cannot be real
Only in marrying your opposite can duality heal

Both your surface self and your shadow will cease to be
Beyond them lies an inseparable reality
The you that is eternally part of the One
Beyond the reaches of duality is that which will come

Twelve goddess archetypes on the Hidden Planets reside
But twelve god archetypes on the Known Planets abide
Upon the Earth the embodiment of the thirteenth goddess forms a
    living gate
When gods and goddesses unite, each becoming one with a mate

The portal of the thirteenth goddess opens and all life goes free
As the illusion falls away of duality
Then all shall flourish in the Being of the One
And a glorious reality to all life shall come

The Song of the 12 God Archetypes

1. *Ranuchserva-hutsvi*   God of pristine glory in action

2. *Blivashnustra-bilestra*   God of peaceful habitations

3. *Nechspu-arastuva*   God of pure cooperation with life

4. *Nasaru-bilechstechvi*   God of the life of no opposites

5. *Belhes-estruva-bilheshtu*   God of clear enlightenment

6. *Pilivet-achvraba-nusvi*   God of endless possibilities

7. *Trives-rasnut-alasvi*   God of fluid expression of divine unfoldment

8. *Araknut-blahasvablu*   God of embracing compassion

9. *Sutret-blaha-estranu*   God of peace and contentment

10. *Kishera-nunanesvi-asta*   God of graceful transitions

11. *Tresharvar-kluvespi*   God of the joy of living

12. *Michpa-eles-stavabi*   God of the rapture of Oneness

The Songs of the 12 God Archetypes

The Planet Selbelechvi

Wheel of Selbelechvi

No matter your choice of paths you traverse, the journey since birth that you travel on Earth, all roads lead up the mountain of timelessness and into the arms of eternity.

Usutablivaves

The group of Angel Gods who serve Selbelechvi

1. *Hasvikiresva*
2. *Usutupares*
3. *Arlechvarsvatu*
4. *Pirech-elesvu*
5. *Arasklubavi*
6. *Araknunas*
7. *Erestrakbar*
8. *Kuresharstu*
9. *Etrek-aravi*
10. *Heleshalasvi*
11. *Kursta-blanut*
12. *Ertrek-nusata*
13. *Ekletberet*
14. *Piras-esetaa*
15. *Aklat-harsvi*
16. *Kuvar-miresat*
17. *Iratvribes*
18. *Esenur-arakla*
19. *Ekresut-halasbi*
20. *Kirstava*
21. *Vilesbrahur*
22. *Inesetre-vravir*
23. *Kurunut-asata*
24. *Piselhur-narsut*

Transmission from Selbelechvi

Seven misalignments that prevent the flow from Source
Hampering our ability to receive eternal resources
From the Dream as a residue they exist
Belief systems of separation that persist

Seven there are that seven directions create
Re-forming matrices and re-creating space
Preventing accessibility to the depth of your being
So that the gates of abundant life open can be

The first belief system that dissolved must be
Is the belief that individuated life ever created has been
Expressions of the One Life that visible seem
That unfold as life throughout all eternity

Uniting opposites that illusion can disappear
Is an effective way for life to be cleared
But the mistaken belief that a shadow an opposite is
Must be cleared – they do not really exist

Each separation, consisting of two poles
Casts a shadow that plays a role
It holds open the space that between poles resides
An effect of duality that disappears when they combine

Many causes of death have already disappeared
But a belief system still lingers that must be cleared
It is thought that the body becomes worn and tired
That it leaves because the soul can no longer in it reside

When life is materialistic and not lived from the soul
It increases in white light and the soul becomes unwhole
When the black light of which the soul is comprised
Is far less than the body's white light

The soul of the body becomes eroded
The soul then flees the body's abode
The same has happened when in the past cosmic cycles closed
Earth as the physical no longer was a hospitable home

It has been thought, mistakenly
That a white light ascension of humanity
Will affect the consciousness of star races directly
For this a feminine ascension is a necessity

Star races have benefited as Earth's consciousness rose
The energy tied up in density was released as frequency rose
This the star races did sustain
But more awareness and understanding was not gained

While disparity between black and white light remains
Incorruptible immortality cannot be maintained
Thus music we bring and movement to replace
Ways of the mind with an ascension of grace

Now it is time for humanity
To see the value of polarity
The gift it brings is the ability
To bring self-appreciation through clarity

No need to see polarity as a curse
See the beauty of life and it will disperse
Belief systems place value on only one pole
Opposites must have equal value for life to be whole

Many belief systems around love and light
Have obscured their true nature from human sight
They are the languages of the head and the heart
Causing illusion between the masculine and feminine parts

The use of languages, it must be seen
A great cause of duality has been
The need is not there to communicate with languages of linearity
When within the One Life there is no duality

The Planet Husvaa

Wheel of Husvaa

The only language anyone hears is the One Life's eternal song. Where only One Being in reality exists, communication does not belong. Communication is part of life's great conspiracy. In order to dance, it pretends duality. (From *The Seer's Journey*)

Ars-kantve-brusat

The group of Angel Gods who serve Husvaa

1. *Keehaa-alna*
2. *Peetre-prahu*
3. *Urustaa-naa*
4. *Paaru-trehaa*
5. *Arlaa-ketre*
6. *Kaarsa-tekpahur*
7. *Erle-erset-arlich*
8. *Kuubaavi-mirset*
9. *Esek-harstaa-eskle*
10. *Eeseeta-arlek*
11. *Harut-ervek-arskla*
12. *Keenee-vraa-steva*

13. *Kaaruutrehutpilva*
14. *Kisetaa-aarut*
15. *Urustek-brusat*
16. *Arakne-veetaa*
17. *Arlavek-breeva*
18. *Rutra-silvavi*
19. *Etrek-baaru*
20. *Kurat-sertuu*
21. *Vivres-arstak*
22. *Peeheesh-nanes*
23. *Ekevee-arstu*
24. *Rutaa-blivek*

Transmission from Husvaa

No more illusions! No more romanticized ideas!
When one regards certain parts of life as more holy, vision becomes
    unclear
Humanity has thought of spirit as the director of their lives
That it must surely be wiser because of its encompassing size

Space and time are two shadows cast by body and soul
When they separated, when they became un-whole
If space does not exist then size is a meaningless idea
It's time for the reality of spirit to be very clear

Spirit is the shadow of another separation
Of the individual's illusion that he is a separate creation
The separation from Source is something that can never be
The spirit forms an individuation – a concept that's illusory

Body and soul, two poles of each other play
When one grows stronger, the other one wanes
Thus polarity is conflict-based
An eternal war that is waged

Live a life that feeds the soul as much as the body is fed
Not one more holy than the other, both treated with respect
To live a life that's purely physical is to be the living dead
With most of the soul depleted and parts that have fled

The Planet Minut

Wheel of Minut

*All comfort zones consist of the familiar and the known whether
one is in ego-identification or the mastery of expansion. Life must
become the unknowable to become One with the Infinite.*
(From *The Seer's Journey*)

Akra-ba-servrut

The group of Angel Gods who serve Minut

1. *Paalabi-ertru*
2. *Ritaa-brevis*
3. *Riskaver-ersklu*
4. *Usaamanes-hursta*
5. *Eekleepeehares*
6. *Uselbarustrahur*
7. *Esetaavaavi*
8. *Veresklaahurparet*
9. *Eretrechvrahur*
10. *Rusetaablaavik*
11. *Rikselvaataaprahur*
12. *Nisatu-blee-es*

13. *Eskebreevranut*
14. *Uklespetrehur*
15. *Utre-miset*
16. *Vrabek-elesvu*
17. *Haastavech*
18. *Kaaruspravata*
19. *Arsna-beeparee*
20. *Eesta-vravee*
21. *Karee-nahespavu*
22. *Usutu-klavahur*
23. *Erestaa-akrahur*
24. *Nunanespelihur*

Transmission from Minut

The animals embody the stages of the Dream
Twenty-four cycles of life that through eons have been
They are not gone, they linger still
Until their value is seen, they always will

They taint the present and perpetuate the past
As long as they aren't balanced their influence will last
The animals bring the lessons they've carried through time
Each carries a message from ages long declined

Learn their insights that old cycles may disappear
That old programs controlling the present may be cleared

The Animal Archetypes of the Dream

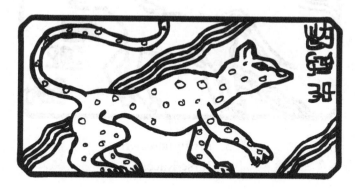

1. *Unach-tu-savaa*
Big Cats

Ascension is the awakening from a dream within a dream

2. *Nanush-bi-sata*
Big Mammals, i.e. elephants

Though the dreams become more lucid, they are still
illusion-based

3. *Bishu-neresva*
Horse Races

Dreams must be understood for the gifts they bring to heal

4. *Kisu-tere-nu*
Antelope and Deer

The dream state and the awakened state are the opposite
poles of one another

5. *Mishapa-situru*
Big Birds, i.e. Ostriches

Anything that can be divided into two poles is not real and eternal

6. *Nestu-hiricsta*
Amphibians

Both poles must be valued equally in order to express equally

7. *Kaarit-ersetu-harech*
Marsupials, i.e. Kangaroo

Poles that express equally can be combined and cancel each
other out

8. *Nechvi-harasat*
Lemurs

If all their parts are balanced and equally combined, only
beingness remains

9. *Sutuvach-barstu*
Apes

The only way to permanently eliminate illusion is through combining its equally expressing poles

10. *Perspa-hisata*
Dog Races – except Wolves

All other methods - like transformation, transmutation, transfiguration – will just re-manifest the illusion in higher and higher forms

11. *Mishera-pirerut*
Wolves

Two opposite poles that exist cast a shadow, which is space

12. *Runarat-aranuk*
Armadillo

The interaction between two poles creates the illusion of
movement, which is time

13. *Sunarut-blivavet*
Domestic and Smaller Cats

When one pole such as the physical body, is over-focused
on, its opposite pole such as the soul, diminishes

14. *Kanavit-erut*
Pigs, Cows, Sheep

The opposites of body and soul cast the shadow called
spirit, or individuation

15. *Kuhus-estravit*
Snakes and Other Reptiles

The animal archetypes represent the 24 dream cycles that
have taken place

16. *Kenevit-arasvi*
Other Mammals

The dream cycles are representative of the 24 hours of the
Earth's rotation

17. *Vrunabit-ruseta*
Water Fowl and Poultry

There are 24 levels of dreaming both cosmically and for all
beings

18. *Asanach-vuhesbi*
Birds of Prey

The animals carry the dream cycles insights, which must
be learned in order to dissolve them for the illusion of
dreaming and awakening to be cancelled out

19. *Klihes-uspenes*
Other Birds

As the cosmos moves to more lucid dreams, old dream cycles do not disappear. They remain as shadows waiting for their value to be seen

20. *Graanit-plubahes*
Bears

Nature has not been purified and evolved as it should since the planetary ascension began[8]

8 In February 2005.

21. *Visinetvi-araskrut*
Marine Life – except Whales

The animals still carry the shadows of previous dream cycles,
known as the cycles of the Fall

22. *Arsa-velebruch-nava*
Whales and Dolphins

The remnants of the 24 dream cycles have also formed the
sub-conscious of the 24 root races and thus affect cosmic life

23. *Kusabit-eleklutvi*
Bees

This creates a past and disturbs cosmic purity by perpetuating memory

24. *Nunusit-plavi*
Other Insects and Spiders

Eliminating dreaming and awakening eliminates all cosmic illusions and is the ultimate cosmic alchemical equation

Healing to Maintain the Health of Animals

Creating the Sacred Space

1. Place the Power Wheel to Maintain the Health and Well-Being of Animals on the bottom of the stack.

2. If the animal is a mammal, place the Animal Totem Wheel for Mammals on top of the Power Wheel.

3. Place the animal's name, picture or the drawing representing the animal on top of the wheel(s).

How to do the Healing

1. Sign (draw) the 24 sigils in the air (while saying their names) over the stack you have prepared with the animal's photo, drawing or name.

2. End by signing (drawing) the remaining 3 sigils and calling the names of the 3 healing angels.

3. Instruct the angels to maintain the health of the animal.

See http://www.kriyavaspata.com/ for further information on healing animals.

The 24 Sigils to Maintain the Health of Animals

Sigil 1

Kaa-ashut-misna

Sigil 2

Bri-abek-vibrasvi

Sigil 3

Pli-avet-miserat

Sigil 4

Kisera-manut

Sigil 5

Serebuch-blasvi

Sigil 6

Misanich-mesarut

Sigil 7

Ach-kanak-niseru

Sigil 8

Nisevra-blivenut

Sigil 9

Silbehut-asklava

Sigil 10

Klibarut-hesvi

Sigil 11

Sakrarut-esekla

Sigil 12

Nuch-barik-sibelut

Sigil 13

Nirevak-uklesvi

Sigil 14

Sekrenisavit

Sigil 15

Etreblanavik

Sigil 16

Pretpra-virinat

Sigil 17

Prubasebarut

Sigil 18

Sitre-miseklut

Sigil 19

Arskla-bivarut

Sigil 20

Vli-unes-askra

Sigil 21

Priseklutmanit

Sigil 22

Sutklepribarut

Sigil 23

Trinamuk-pliva

Sigil 24

Kershkla-bluves

The Angels for Healing Animals

Angel Sigil 1:

Sitremiserut

Angel Sigil 2:

Areruk-usekli

Angel Sigil 3:

Pirenut-hareklet

Animal Totem Wheel for Mammals

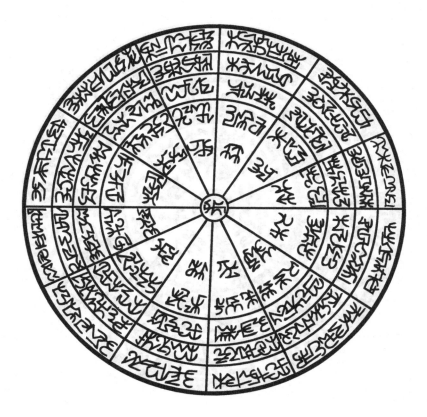

The Power Wheel to Maintain the Health and Well-being of Animals

Kushana Harasvi Erekla

Closing

The transmissions from these Hidden Planets have indicated a profound reverence for life and an inspiring depth of perception. It has become clear after translating over a thousand pages of transmissions from star races that humans have the most latent power at their disposal, but not the perception needed to wield it.

In bringing their gifts of insights to humanity; insights and knowledge held for eons in anticipation of the dawn of consciousness on Earth, this innate power of man can now become accessible. Let us receive it with the grateful acknowledgement it deserves.

With love, praise and gratitude,

Almine

Appendix

Equation to Heal the Polarity of the Dream State and the Awakened State

The balancing of all dream and awakened cycles

+

The uniting of all dream and awakened cycles

+

The eliminating of all dream and awakened state shadows

=

The Holy marriage of opposites to close the cycles of duality

Power Square to Balance All Opposite Poles

Power Wheel to Join All Opposites

Kunach Piravet Minachvi

Related Products by Almine

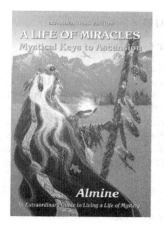

A Life of Miracles

Expanded Third Edition Includes Bonus Belvaspata Section, Mystical Keys to Ascension

A Life of Miracles tells of Almine's developing spiritual awareness and abilities from her childhood in South Africa until she emerged as a powerful mystic, to devote her gifts in support of all humanity. Deeply inspiring and unique in its comparison of man's relationship as the microcosm of the macrocosm. *Also available in Spanish*

Published: 2009, 304 pages, soft cover, 6 x 9, ISBN: 978-1-934070-25-3

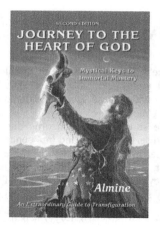

Journey to the Heart of God Second Edition

Mystical Keys to Immortal Mastery

Ground-breaking cosmology revealed for the first time, sheds new light on previous bodies of information such as the Torah, the I Ching and the Mayan Zolkien. The explanation of man's relationship as the microcosm as set out in the previous book A Life of Miracles, is expanded in a way never before addressed by New Age authors, giving new meaning and purpose to human life. Endorsed by an Astrophysicist from Cambridge University and a former NASA scientist, this book is foundational for readers at all levels of spiritual growth.

Published: 2009, 276 pages, soft cover, 6 x 9, ISBN: 978-1-934070-26-0

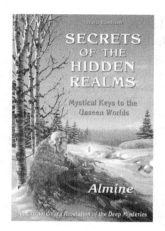

Secrets of the Hidden Realms
Third Edition
Mystical Keys to the Unseen Worlds

This remarkable book delves into mysteries few mystics have ever revealed. It gives in detail:
> The practical application of the Goddess mysteries
> Secrets of the angelic realms
> The maps, alphabets, numerical systems of
> Lemuria, Atlantis, and the Inner Earth
> The Atlantean calendar, accurate within 5 minutes
> The alphabet of the Akashic libraries.

Secrets of the Hidden Realms amazing bridge across the chasm that has separated humanity for eons from unseen realms.

Published: 2011, 412 pages, soft cover, 6 x 9, ISBN: 978-1-936926-38-1

Related Products by Almine

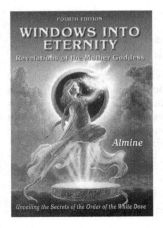

Windows into Eternity
Revelations of the Mother Goddess

This book provides unparalleled insight into ancient mysteries. Almine, an internationally recognized mystic and teacher, reveals the hidden laws of existence. Transcending reason, delivering visionary expansion, this metaphysical masterpiece explores the origins of life as recorded in the Holy Libraries. The release of information from these ancient libraries is a priceless gift to humankind. The illusions found in the building blocks of existence are exposed, as are the purposes of Creation.

Published 2011, 309 pages, soft cover, 6 x 9, ISBN 978-1-936929-26-8

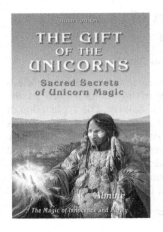

Gift of the Unicorns
Sacred Secrets of Unicorn Magic, 3rd Edition NEW

Where have the Unicorns gone? And, what about mystical winged horses, mermaids, and giants – do they exist? The answers to all of our questions about these fabled creatures can be found in The Gift of the Unicorns.

This magical book tells the story of the Unicorns and Pegasus, and their heroism in preserving purity and innocence during the ages of darkness on Earth. In their own words, these beings reveal where they went, the purpose of their golden shoes and the sacred mission they undertook for the Mother of All Creation. What's more, they share long-held secrets about the Earth.

Published: 2012, 188 pages, soft cover, 6 x 9, ISBN: 978-1-936926-48-0

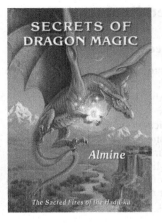

Secrets of Dragon Magic
The Sacred Fires of the Hadji-ka

This extraordinary record of the philosophy and practices of dragon magic is unmatched in its depth of knowledge and powerful delivery. From the Sacred Records of the Hadji-ka, kept by the dragons of Avondar, the secrets of Kundalini are revealed, designed to restore the innate, natural magical abilities of man lost by the separation of the spinal column and the pranic tube. The reader is swept along on a profound and mystical journey that pushes perception beyond mortal boundaries. Almine's infallible ability to empower her reading audience is clearly felt throughout the pages of this book.

Published: 2013, 418 pages, soft cover, 6 x 9, ISBN: 978-1-936926-56-5

Related Products by Almine

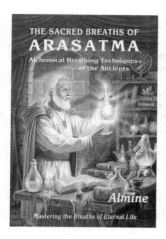

The Sacred Breaths of Arasatma
Alchemical Breathing Techniques of the Ancients
Mastering the Breaths of Eternal Life

The Arasatma breathing techniques were used by ancient mystics to activate the unused portion of the pranic tube. This facilitates fuller self-expression and inner peace.

The restoration of the subtle, etheric functions of the body and senses allows the practitioner to access other dimensions and prolongs an eternal life of graceful unfolding.

Includes download of 1½ hour accompanying music.

Published: 2013, 386 pages, soft cover, 6 x 9, ISBN 978-1-936926-64-0

Seer's Wisdom
Guidance for Spiritual Mastery

Immerse yourself in the true nature of your being: Abundant living. This book shows you how to access your natural abundance and remove all blockages of flow. It is packed with over 400 pages of classic Almine aphorisms. Seer's Wisdom reminds you of the benign source of your own being and focuses your attention on attaining abundance: Abundance in yourself, abundance in your environment, abundance in your relationships and much more.

"To live within the Infinite's Being is to live in the fullness of an inexhaustible supply. Acknowledging the never-ending Source of abundance increases its accessibility."

Published: 2013, 430 pages, soft cover, 6 x 9, ISBN: 978-1-936926-52-7

Music by Almine

Alchemy of Sound

As one of the leading mystics and alchemists on Earth today, Almine employs techniques of alchemical potencies of sound to neutralize illusion in your environment.

By combining what is known to mystics as frequencies of white light with those of black light, illusions such as lack, aging and disease, can be canceled out. Alchemists have long known that when the null point is reached, the full potential of the body can be accessed.

Children of the Sun

Music from the Known Planets (Re-mastered and re-titled version of the Interstellar Sound Elixirs)

The beautiful interstellar sound elixirs received and sung by Almine.

Price $9.95 MP3 Download
$14.95 CD

Labyrinth of the Moon

Music from the Hidden Planets (Re-titled version of the Sound Elixirs of the Hidden Planets)

All the vocals in these elixirs are received and sung in the moment by Almine

Price $9.95 MP3 Download
$14.95 CD

Jubilation - Songs of Praise

Music from around the world to lift the heart and inspire the listener.

The extraordinary mystical quality of the music, and the exquisite clarity of Almine's voice, creates the ambient impression of being in the presence of angels.

Price $9.95 MP3 Download
$14.95 CD

Additional Products by Almine

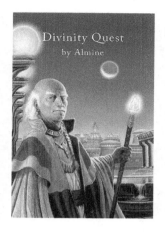

Divinity Quest

Through ages of existence of cycles of life, death and ascension, there are those great lights on Earth who have felt the deep anguish of knowing that the reality of man is not their own; that a higher reality beckons. Almine has laid down a map for the magnificent journey home to the greater reality of godhood.

Divinity Quest is a physical card deck for divination and DNA activation. It's an easy yet profound tool, enabling the remembrance and activation of your divine origin in daily life.

Price $34.95

Elfin Quest

The 60 cards of Elfin Quest have many important roles to play in your life. They are not only a source of daily guidance and inspiration, but also a sacred tool to evolve consciousness and facilitate healing. The healing protocol included with the card deck, allows the life force to flow unimpeded through the spine to increase the vitality present in various parts of the body. Elfin Quest is a powerful and life altering tool, brought to you by the leading mystic of our time.

Price $34.95

CPSIA information can be obtained at www.ICGtesting.com
Printed in the USA
BVOW08s1805240814

364047BV00012B/218/P